The Mental Guide for The Average Golfer

The Mental Guide for The Average Golfer

Horace L. Mitchell

Copyright© 2024. Horace L. Mitchell. All Rights Reserved.

No part of this work covered by the copyright herein may be reproduced or used in any form or by any means—graphic, electronic, or mechanical without the prior written permission of the publisher. Any request for photocopying, recording, taping, or information storage and retrieval systems of any part of this book shall be directed in writing to the author.

This publication contains the opinions and ideas of its author(s) and is designed to provide useful advice in regard to the subject matter covered.

Inquiries and Book Orders should be addressed to:

Writer's Torch Press & Media
Email: admin@writerstorch.com
Phone: 347-768-7550

Printed in the United States of America

ISBN: 979-8-89175-125-5 (hc)

Disclaimer

The Mental Guide is just what it says; this publication is or was not written to coach the golfer to swing, nor break down anything other than the mental approach needed to improve another level of mental clarity of their ability to "Score," using these three components:

- Attitude
- Aptitude
- Execution

DEDICATION

This has been the hardest part to write. There are so many along the way, and it is an effort not to overlook anyone. First, this book is dedicated to my brother, Even Mitchell, whose mentorship I have always treasured, not just as a brother but as a man. I must give credit to my loving wife, Vivian Mitchell, for allowing me to experience this beautiful journey.

Without her love and support, I am sure this would be a different story. My eternal friend and playing companion, Mr. Fernando Francis (Cinco), has played an especially important part in the knowledge we acquired from our many years as playing partners. He also encouraged me to begin instructing twenty-five years prior. To my daughter, Tamara Mitchell, for sending me to the Hollywood Golf Institute's junior program, acknowledging the talent she knew I had with children. I must make this a dual dedication, if not for my departed friend and associate, Mr. Jessie Jacobs Jr., for the insightful assistance that led to the success achieved with the Hollywood Golf Institute's students. To see them "Blossom" has to be one of the "Wonders" of this world.

Finally, for being allowed by Mrs. Selina Johnson to incorporate this system of Attitude, Aptitude, and Execution into the training format. The program and staff taught Jessie and me the true meaning of empathy and dedication to educating the children.

I am so "Grateful!"

Expressions of Appreciation

Elliott Tabron
Mr. Horace Mitchell, a.k.a. "Jim Dent," is probably the greatest golf coach I have ever met. I say that because he teaches his students the most valuable lesson in golf, which is how to score and how to play the game mentally as well as physically. He is responsible for my game going from the mid-90s to the mid-70s. Might I say, much faster than anticipated, he coached me while I was living in Detroit but continued my mental training over the phone once I moved to Arizona. In summation, his book should help any golfer who is or has been seeking an elevation in the mental phase of their game. An alarming thing happens because of the new stage of awareness: his book unlocks the golfer's approach and is dramatically redirected for the better.

This book is a must-read.

Thank you! (Dent)

Joe Journey PGA, CHG
Horace Mitchell, my inaugural golf coach, known as Mr. Dent, has profoundly illuminated my journey toward achieving the esteemed titles of Class A PGA Professional, Tour Player, and Master Golf Instructor. The significance of this book resonates not just within my personal trajectory but will reverberate indefinitely throughout the entire realm of golf.

Thank you!

Horace L. Mitchell

Jameel Lockhart
I am incredibly grateful for the transformative impact Horace Mitchell has had on my game. From my early years as a kid to becoming a scratch golfer, he has been a guiding force throughout my junior, college, and amateur golf journey. His expertise not only refined my technical skills but also instilled a winning mindset crucial for success in the competitive realm of golf.

His commitment extends beyond personal achievements; my coach has played a pivotal role in shaping the golfing landscape for hundreds of kids in the Detroit area and beyond. His ability to nurture talent and cultivate a passion for the sport is unparalleled. His coaching transcends mere skill development; it is about fostering a love for the game and building character through the challenges golf presents.

I attribute my growth as a golfer to his unwavering support, insightful guidance, and dedication to honing the skills of aspiring golfers. His influence has created a lasting impact not only on my game but on the broader golf community. I wholeheartedly recommend him to anyone seeking not just a coach but a mentor who genuinely cares about their journey in the world of golf.

Thank you!

Micheal Horner
My longtime friend DENT.

We started playing golf in 1974 together. We were competitors.

But we were friends at first.

He was truly a phenomenal young gentleman. He has a passion for others working with young people. He has the heart of a lion and take-no-prisoners. He knows who he is. He truly was one no-nonsense player. But we did have fun. A lot of times, we would laugh at the matches. Win or lose? Then, back at each other tomorrow. He stayed committed to all his golf shots. That is why he was such a phenomenal putter, chipper, and all-around player. Like I said, we were competitive, but we are truly friends. Congratulations Dent. Keep being the great person that you are.

Rayan Jerome
Before I write about who I am here to tell you about, let me tell you a bit about myself. I recently turned 40 years old, and I have been golfing off and on since I was 13 years old. I had never played an actual round of golf until I went to my first year of high school and tried out for the golf team. Crazy, right? Going to try out for the golf team and had only practiced with my uncle around the yard a few times. Well, I went for the first tryout and my first time on the golf course. I played my 9-hole round, and at the end, they said I shot a "42." I could not believe how well I played for the first time. Long story short, I went on to be the #1 varsity seat in my first and sophomore years of high school. I was even awarded Rookie of the Year. My best round ever played in high school was 71, 35 on the front, and 36 on the back -1 under par. Ever since my short-lived high school career, I had never had any formal lessons from anyone. I picked my golf game back up in my late 20s. My extreme love for the game locked me back in, and I was hooked for life. As was stated before, I was on and off with my game, but this was all due to life. Finally, in 2015, I was able to start focusing on my game again, and it was the only thing I spent my days doing. I had a passion from the first time I picked up a golf club at 13 to become a professional player on the PGA Tour. I met Mr. Horrace Mitchell, a.k.a "Dent," in 2015 at a driving range located in Southfield, Michigan. I had been at this driving range every day for the past three months.

Horace L. Mitchell

Dent had seen me at the range swinging as powerfully and fast as I could, knocking the balls as far out of the park as I could. Sure, most of them were going out there, and then some were not. I had really forgotten how I had played in high school and was now trying to unlock all the potential I knew I had. I saw the beginning of it when I was young, but as they say, if you do not use it, you will lose it. No matter what, I was hell-bent on unlocking the door to my ability. When Dent approached me at the range, I really did not have the best attitude. I never took lessons, and I did not feel I needed them, but I still had an open ear, and what I was hearing from Dent began to take hold and made me more intrigued about his knowledge. After a few hours with Dent, I realized that he was authentic. To this day, I still call him "The Golf Guru." Wow! I have realized so much in this brief period of learning with Dent. I have become a true student of what he is enlightening me on this trip. Mr. Dent said he teaches "Attitude, Aptitude, and Execution, along with a very specific 5-step routine." All I have to say is, "Wow!" The routine is so deep and reveals so much over time. I cannot begin to explain in this short expression Mr. Dent and the knowledge he truly possesses. There are so many levels to the journey I am on, with the routine and what it has truly shown me about myself and how to get out of my own way and allow what needs to happen effortlessly. I had more life to come up, but after one year with Dent, I had to take a 6-year hiatus from my game. I know how depressing and so much time off I was losing away from my quest. Fast forward to summer 2023; baby, I am back, and the routine was still with me, just a bit forgotten and not as familiar to me anymore, but man, I was golfing well, or so I thought. Having an issue with my driver, I said, "Man, what am I doing? I need to call Dent right away." I knew I had to get back with him to continue my training. Folks, this brings us to now January 2024 after a short time back, Mr. Dent, and I, I don't even know how to explain to you how quickly and

The Mental Guide for The Average Golfer

how deep the journey has been into my understanding of the game, myself and my focus on how to continue to remove the chains that had locked up my potential for so long. The epiphanies, the many epiphanies. I am now headed to Florida to play in my first professional tournament on Feb 28th. This journey is just beginning, and I can only pray God will allow this beautiful journey to continue. I have truly walked through the door of enlightenment and have been made aware of what it takes to become the best I can be. No matter where you are in your game, Mr. Dent, the Golf Guru, truly has knowledge that you just will not believe, but it takes truly paying attention and, without question, doing exactly as instructed, no matter what you think. If you do not yet believe it, try it, and I can guarantee you will have the best golf game and you will be able to play for life. Mr. Dent, my Golf Guru, thank you, sir, for all that you have done for me and my golf career. You have truly given me the tools to continue to excel in my game as it will always continue to improve, for the routine is everything. I know anyone who reads *The Mental Guide for The Average Golfer* will improve their mental performance, and his book will resonate throughout the golf world.

Thank you!

A.C. Burks

Horace Mitchell (Dent) has been a friend for he has a strong character and unwavering loyalty. Dent possesses a winning attitude that rivals the greats in professional sports. We met on the course over 30 years ago. During that time, there were epic battles between the two of us, and we also played matches as partners. He never gives up; once, in a match at "Fox Creek Golf Course," we were on the par five 18th hole. Dent's third shot was adjacent to the green in knee-tall grass, on the short side thirty yards away. My playing partners Chris and Poole, along with myself, were in perfect position to

Horace L. Mitchell

birdie the hole, so there was no worry that we had won the hole. Well, all we saw was Dent take the swing grass fly, the ball lob high into the air onto the green and into the hole! Dent then alerted us to the fact that that was for "FOUR." Needless to say, not one of us made birdie. Working with the children, he has a true talent. He also has a unique teaching style; you will know one of his students anywhere they are because he knows the true flaws within the golfer's swing, and the ability to recognize talent makes him a great educator. I like watching the students' consistent routine and powerful swings like the pendulum on a clock; the routine never changes. Dent's other traits are mental toughness and a "Bulldog" attitude once his opponent is down. In my formative years, I was well-practiced and prepared to win the "Horton Smith"/Michigan Medal Play Public Links Invitational annual tournament. I knew I needed to have a good caddy, so I asked Dent if he would consider carrying my bag in the "Horton Smith?" The reply I received was, "Are you going to 'win?'"

"Of course," I answer, "but I need a good caddy, and I trust you." Once committed, I knew he was the proper one, and as it turned out, more so than I anticipated. At breakfast, the morning of sitting with one of the golfers who knew me well, asked aloud, "A.C., who do you like in the tournament?" Dent rose and announced to the room that it would be me. When I tugged him down to the seat because I was embarrassed, Dent asked if I knew that we came to "Win?" I reluctantly answered yes, but after that day with my friend on the bag, I learned what a true winning attitude is. Because of the strength and unwavering belief Dent had in me gave me the intestinal fortitude to "Win." He is the guy you could leave your wallet and jewelry with while you go swimming. Dent is so trustworthy, and if you were to walk down a dark alley, he is the guy you want on your side. For the golfers who need help with the game, Dent has been the instructor to see.

He does not try to change or rebuild the swing, no! He only strengthens the knowledge of the fundamentals to increase the club head speed by creating better "balance" through the swing. The true value is his ability to make the student recognize the importance of the "tempo," which is the basis of any solid swing. To date, I have yet to come across anyone who can create mental strength in their student like Dent. His philosophy is golf is only 15 percent physical and 85 percent mental. Take heed of his scoring theory using the mental approach aired in his book; I am sure you will improve. I have always sought his advice.

Do well, my friend.

Phil Smith

Horace Mitchell has been a friend for over forty years. We affectionately call him Dent because of his ability to hit the driver a long distance, like Jim Dent, who led the PGA Tour in driving distance for several years consecutively and was an African American on the PGA Tour the year Dent began golf. Horace was a very clutch and cerebral player. He had the mentality to pull off the appropriate golf shot in any situation. He has a positive attitude. The glass is always half full, not half empty. Horace and I played a golf match against Bobby Stroble and Jimmy Westley, without any doubt. Horace's attitude and shot-making ability were paramount to our winning the match against the two PGA touring professionals. Yeah, we tied the front and destroyed them on the back nine. This book, *The Mental Guide for the Average Golfer*, will illuminate the importance of opening the "Attitude" to allow the growth necessary. This book suddenly takes a different approach.

My Friend ("Dent.")

Horace L. Mitchell

Bobby Lawrence
Our thoughts and emotions have a significant impact on our lives beyond the tangible. Coach Dent has advised me to have faith in the process and not to interfere. Trust the routine and add the tempo to create consistency. I am confident the content of this book will clear up questions that seemed unanswerable. The routine, along with the mental approach aired in this publication, supersede any information I have found that educates the students with an innovative style and charismatic personality that has been transferred to print. This is a must-read for any golfer questing to improve.

Thanks "Coach Dent."

Turner S. Thompson
Horace Mitchell is the perfect person to author a book on the mental game of golf. I play over 300 rounds of golf every year, pain-free because of the concepts and techniques learned from Horace. He teaches the mental and physical aspects of golf, recognizing that having a routine can make the difference between playing a good round of golf and having a great round! I still use and share with others the routines Horace taught me, especially for the short game, pitching, chipping, and putting – where the game is won. I have referred many beginning golfers and some others who just want to improve their game to Mr. Mitchell. I will also recommend this book to anyone who loves the game of golf or is interested in learning.

Keep doing what you do!

John Wallace (J DUB)
Dent has been one of the best teachers in my over 40 years of playing golf. His passion and mental insight helped propel my game to new heights. In fact, after reconnecting with Dent over the last three years, I have since won three golf tournaments, including the Club Championship at TPC of

Dearborn. This book describes in detail all the important points and techniques Dent has taught me that have led to Wins. Thank you, Dent, for all your help, and good luck with your book.

Do well, "Coach!"

Norris Brown Jr.
Head Educator/Instructor

Hollywood Golf Institute Inc.

Unlocking Golf Excellence: A Journey with Horace Mitchell has not been just as a golf instructor but a meaningful change to the approach. Under his tutelage, golf transcends the mere act of swinging a club – it becomes an art form, a passion, and a journey of self-discovery.

What sets Mr. Mitchell apart is his unwavering commitment to his students' success. From the moment you step onto the course with him, you know you are in the presence of someone who genuinely cares about your improvement and growth as a golfer. His dedication goes beyond technical instruction; he delves into the nuances of the game, understanding that success in golf requires mastering both the physical and mental aspects.

With Horace, it is not just about perfecting your swing – though he is certainly a master of swing mechanics. It is about unlocking your true potential as a golfer. He tailors his instruction to suit your individual strengths, weaknesses, and goals, guiding you with patience, expertise, and an infectious enthusiasm for the game.

But Horace's greatest gift lies in his ability to instill confidence. He does not just teach you how to swing a club; he teaches

Horace L. Mitchell

you how to believe in yourself, how to approach each shot with focus and determination, and how to overcome obstacles with grace and resilience. Under his guidance, you become not only a better golfer but also a stronger, more confident individual.

Horace Mitchell is not just a golf instructor – he is a mentor, a motivator, and a true ambassador for the sport. Whether you are a beginner taking your first swings or a seasoned pro looking to fine-tune your game, Horace's wisdom, passion, and expertise will undoubtedly leave a lasting impact on your journey toward golf excellence.

Fernando Francis (Cinco)

It is a pleasure and honor to acknowledge to the world that my playing partner and friend, Mr. Horace Mitchell, is airing to the public what I have seen over the many years. Being a skillful player myself, it is hard to see the true talent that someone else has until their performance illuminates itself to the point it cannot be denied. Mr. Mitchell (Dent) has, over the years, shown me the three facets of this publication that has been written. His "Attitude" truly supersedes any level of the competition we have played, and he has had the ability to transfer the playing approach of "Attitude, Aptitude, and Execution" to the students he instructs with an unequaled pace. Over the years, his unwavering commitment to his routine and willingness to continue to elevate his ability to score has always been the reasons for my confidence in winning the competitions we have entered over the years. Mr. Mitchell (Dent) and I have both been blessed to have been friends, business associates, and playing partners for more than 30 years. I am convinced that *The Mental Guide for The Average Golfer* is a must-read, and the way the reader looks at improving their game will be changed forever.

This is an "Honor," my friend!

Contents

Foreword by Selena Johnson 1

Insight 3

Introduction 5

Attitude 9

Aptitude 11

Execution 15

Thank You Note 33

Foreword by Selena Johnson

In the world of golf, where the whisper of the wind can carry as much weight as the swing of a club, I have had the unparalleled privilege of being mentored by someone whose voice has been both a guiding whisper and a resonant force in my journey. For over two decades, we have walked the greens, navigated the bunkers, and celebrated the birdies under the tutelage of a mentor whose approach to golf—and life—is as impactful as his personality is indelible.

Bluntness, passion, and a strong personality might read as mere adjectives to an outsider, but for those of us fortunate enough to have been enveloped in his world, they are the very foundation upon which we have built our understanding and appreciation of this timeless sport. His straightforwardness, a beacon in the fog, cuts through the complexities and uncertainties of golf, leaving in its wake clarity and a heightened sense of purpose. His passion, meanwhile, is infectious; it is a flame that lights up the darkest of days, reminding us why we fell in love with golf in the first place. And his strong personality? It is the glue that binds it all together, a testament to the unwavering commitment and resilience required not just to play golf but to excel at it.

This book, a culmination of years of wisdom, experience, and, above all, a deep love for golf, is not just an instructional manual; it is a manifesto of what it means to truly understand the heart and soul of this sport. Through its pages, you will find not just techniques and strategies but life lessons that extend well beyond the fairway. You will hear the voice of someone who has not only mastered the game but has also dedicated his life to teaching others how to find their own path to mastery.

As you turn each page, I encourage you to read not just with your eyes but with your heart. Embrace the bluntness; it is there to sharpen your focus. Let the passion ignite your own love for the game; it is a gift that keeps on giving.

CEO: Hollywood Golf Institute Inc.

INSIGHT

Horace L. Mitchell, born Dec 03, 1946, son of Evans and Geneva Mitchell, in the town of Bastrop, Louisiana that is in Morehouse Parish, northern end of the state. I never considered playing golf as a teenager. I tried to caddy once but did not like it at all. I relocated to Detroit in 1969 and started playing golf in 1974 while working for "GM Proving Grounds" in Milford, Michigan. I was test-driving cars at midnight, so I was getting off at 8 a.m. in the morning. The traffic was always murderous, especially in the winter. Once at home, I would call and talk with my girlfriend just to kill time until I was sleepy while being bored and not sleepy. After a brief time, I was asked not to call her anymore because she was working. At that point, she suggested I go over to "Stacy's Driving Range," which was located in front of the racetrack that we often attended. For some reason, I assumed it was the little cars for it to be a Driving Range. No, it turned out to be a golf driving range, but Since I made the trip over, I might as well knock all the balls away. From that day at Stacy's Driving Range, I knew this was something that had gotten my interest but had no idea it would be for a "lifetime." At the beginning of my golf experience, I started at "Plamer Park Golf Course" the center of "African American" golf in the city of Detroit, Michigan. In no time, I was meeting a lot of prominent people and all the stars from "Motown Records" who were golfers, plus doctors, lawyers, and city officials. Through the many years and the early days at "Palmer Park" one of the things I am truly

Horace L. Mitchell

thankful for is that 99% of the Black Professionals, no matter if they were on the "PGA Tour" or "CHITTERLING Tour," all came to Palmer Park Golf Course. Meeting these "Great Black Golfers" really inspired me. Once I became a "student" of the game, the quest for "Knowledge" began. It is said that those who can do and those who cannot teach. The mental facet of this game is what I found that makes the game of golf so challenging. It is the "Chess Game" of "Life.

The game of golf changed my entire life and the concept of attacking problems head-on. It is a privilege to put in print what has helped me along the way.

Horace l. Mitchell

(DENT)

12/30/2023

INTRODUCTION

After beginning to play golf in 1974 at the age of 28, at "Palmer Park Golf Course," I never thought of the possibility of obtaining the level of knowledge and playing skills. Golf had to be the furthest thing from my mind. This is why a person never knows where he/she will end up once the journey begins or what end or heights the trip will take them. After being sent to the driving range by my then-girlfriend and now my wife, the journey began. Stacy's Driving Range was the place where the first ball was struck, and I found out that I would be playing this game for life. It was no time at all I realized that this was a game that warranted a different attitude and approach. It took some time to understand what the reason was for me not getting better, but it never came into focus until I was forced to move up in competition to become better. Seeing, looking, and watching does not mean that what is being learned is proper. I spent too much of my time trying to learn how to hit the ball instead of learning just the opposite: how to get it in the hole. This is when I stumbled upon what turned out to be the key: my "Attitude;" it was not allowing me to grow. Once I was able to correct and control my "Attitude," things began to take a turn for the better. The game of golf has parallels with life; everything matters, and there are no insignificant things. The next thing that became apparent was even though I had gotten my "Attitude" in check, my scores did not reflect as much positive effect as I expected. This is the reason playing with stronger competitors makes you stronger. It is what was revealed and had to be the next phase of enlightenment.

Horace L. Mitchell

The knowledge of what the better players were capable of was far beyond my mind. Bingo, another light came on: "Aptitude;" this was the point I had to understand that I could not do anything I did not know.

Every time I thought I had found the right information, I was disappointed and disillusioned and could only argue with others about whether what was being done was "Right or Wrong," but whether I won or lost, I was not improving. From that point, I never argued golf again. I found that once anyone obtains the "Proper" information, everything starts to head in the direction I was seeking. I had solved two pieces of a puzzle. Now, I had to take that enlightened "Attitude" and "Aptitude" to the course.

The most astonishing thing happened because I took everything I had practiced, including "Expectation," to the course.

At the time, I did not know that "Expectation" was the killer of "Dreams" and "Murder" to further advancement. There lies "The Wall!" This is where the "Average" golfer is stuck with no clue how to proceed and develops a substandard approach to achieving the ability to score. This golfer will settle for his skill set staying on that level. I learned that in the "Execution" phase it is strictly about using the information learned in the latter stages.

Once committed, I learned to create personal inward awareness of how to stay out of the way.

In this publication, it is my sincere hope that anyone who reads this book will come away with the knowledge within this text and open the door to the ability to lower his/her score.

- ATTITUDE
- APTITUDE
- EXECUTION

"I see it as a blind man; I know it as a fool. Understanding can only be clear once I change my "Attitude!" H.L.M

By far, these three components in the game of golf far exceed any other criteria used and will create the consistency each golfer is looking for.

Horace L. Mitchell

(Dent)

Attitude

Attitude" is by far the major key to opening the "Portal" to the beginning of the journey and the understanding of the "Mission." Until the "Attitude" opens to allow the individual to truly see and admit to themselves that I am not all that and a piece of bubble gum, there just might be proper information out there.

The "Attitude" also deals with one's ability to absorb and maintain information. The first stage of learning. This is truly the first stage of learning to "Focus." Until this phase, he/she starts to understand how much information he/she was not aware of; he/she was not paying enough attention and is unaware of steps being overlooked throughout the proper "Set-Up" process. The "Attitude" must keep the mind "Positive" to keep the golfer's mind from "Freezing Up" so his/her game can come around at the rate the golfer is seeking. A "Positive Attitude" always has a "Positive Effect" on not only one's golf game but also one's life. There is an impossibility to archive the true height of one's ability without a "Positive Attitude.' This is the difference between growing with each loss or failed incident and using that experience as a learning tool instead of a defeat. Understanding that the loss of one battle does not mean the war is over. (It has just begun).

Horace L. Mitchell

From my observation, there are three types of "Attitudes":

- Shy/Unsure: This person will only use golf for recreation and fun.
- Quiet/Demur: This golfer is mostly more focused and interested in becoming more efficient.
- Open/Bold: This golfer will and can carry their game to the height they are willing to practice.

Understand, the thing that is unique to the game of golf is the fact that it is a "Right-Handed" game, played from the "Left," which makes it "Backward." In summation, the reason for the disconnect begins from the beginning once a person makes their mind up to take up the game. Their mental approach will be to attack learning golf in the same manner everything has been learned, so it is normal for him/her to be totally confused and distorted until he/she finds out, "Is this something I really want to do?" The students who seem to be the most challenging are the ones who are blessed with natural athletic ability or super intelligence. In my span of instructing male/female, the ratio in this respect is about even.

In this stage of enlightenment, he/she must come to grips with "Self" and concentrate on staying "Positive." It is the only way to keep calm and the mind open. Since "Attitude" is the controller of his/her ability to stay focused and keep the golfer from overthinking or overdoing, the "Proper Attitude" will and can allow the golfer to pay attention to the knowledge acquired from the work put in. Along with the "Tempo," these are the components that allow him/her to maintain the "Calm and Alertness" required to produce the consistency he/she is seeking.

The "Proper Attitude" works throughout one's life and inspires a "Winning Attitude" that spills over into everything else.

Stay Positive!

Aptitude

This level of information must deal with "Paying Attention" and only obtaining the "Proper Information." No longer dealing with "Right or Wrong," neither word has anything to do with golf. In fact, the words "Right or Wrong" are one of the reasons "The Average Golfer" spends so much time looking for answers to a problem that he/she creates themselves. "Right or Wrong" is nothing but an "Argument," even with yourself, that is difficult to win. The only way to know that the knowledge obtained, no matter the source or area of expertise, is "Results." The "Results" is and should be how information is rated. When the "Proper Information" has been gotten, the results will appear. Through this phase, he/she must "Focus" on the creation of a "Routine" to have reference points for creating the "Proper" setup and posture required to hit each shot. Since the "Average Golfer" has more than likely never had any formal instruction from a qualified golf instructor, this information should be valuable to him/her in the quest to improve his/ her ability to score. The "Aptitude" must only deal with information that is proven from the "Positive" results obtained from hours and hours of endless practice. Please do not kid yourself and do not "Accept" anything less than the results he/she is seeking. I am amiss to say there are a host of reasons the "Proper Information" in this game is hard to come by. This is the reason for this publication. Gaining a strong knowledge of anything (not just golf.) is attributed to how "Open" and Receptive the mind is to receive "Different" forms of information. Whether he/she realizes it or not, when the "Proper work" work is put in, the "positive" results will appear.

The "Aptitude" can only maintain a high level of information retention once the "Attitude" has been opened to allow the "Proper Information" to be obtained and allow the data to materialize in the performance on the course. The creation of the "Routine" is "Optimum" to achieve any form of "Consistency" and also begins to train oneself to become "Left Eye dominant," setting up the "Club Head" off the "Left Heel." This is the phase where all the attention must be paid to "Detail," for the last time understanding that "Everything" matters. There are no "Insignificant" things in golf or life. This is the stage of "Enlightenment" and "Understanding" of the "Mental" importance that is required to reach the level of "Focus" demanded. Very few athletes ever realize for a long time in his/her training that it takes focus to learn how to focus, but, in this life, there are levels to everything. The "Aptitude" is truly the "Key" to entering that door and also "Keeping" the door open to his/her future. (You cannot do what you do not know.). In this phase, he/she must be aware of not getting "Hung-Up or Trapped" into believing, as the advancement of the performance improves, that "I've Got It." You will never have another good shot that day playing or practicing.

Since "Consistency" is the common ground between being good or the best he/she can be, it also allows him/her to introduce the "Glue," which is the "Tempo." Throughout learning the learning process, it is imperative that he/she work with the development of a "Tempo" from the "Putter" to the "Driver."

Because golf deals with angles, it becomes difficult to wrap the mind around the fact that to just establish decent scoring,

The Mental Guide for The Average Golfer

a golf game takes hours and hours of practice, practice, and more practice, and that is just to become decent. The level of information obtained and the amount of practice will dictate the growth of the course.

Knowledge is "KING!"

Execution

The "Execution" phase is the one that makes the golfer realize the growth in each, and everything ascertained in the first and second parts of the scoring mental approach. The true awareness of how open the "Attitude" was is how much information was transferred into the consistency and confidence the golfer is seeking. In this, the true quest is to take everything learned and practiced to the course. During this phase, the truth is taking place. First, "Expectation" must be eliminated. From this point in the golf experience, he/she must not "Expect" anything, just "Go See!" Seeking to become better at golf, the only thing that reveals how far he/she is away is to put it to the test. The stronger the competition in every stage of one's development on the course, it will identify the components being missed or need strengthening in the "Routine and Set-Up" that is not in "Sync" with the sequencing of his/her "Routine." The two common disconnects in the "Average Golfer's," "Routine and "Set-Up."

A: Not training himself/herself to be "Left Eye" dominant.

B: Not watching or paying enough attention to the movement of the "Right Foot" placement off the left heel in the "Set-Up."

At this point, he/she is not confident of the "Ball Placement," and there lies the beginning of the end. Bending over from the waist until the chest is facing the ground, then and only then can the golfer "Set-Up" properly to strike the shot.

The "Balance" is the most important facet of the entire learning process. It is an impossibility to be proficient or efficient in any sport when the "Balance" is not under control. Then and only then will he/she begin to filter through the mountains of "Misinformation" obtained over the extent of his/her golf experience.

No true commitment can or should be made until his/her "Balance" is intact. This, along with the "Tempo," makes the golfer stronger and more confident, from the "Putter" to" the "Driver." Since this is dealing with the "Mental" aspect, keeping his/herself in the process is the reason the body can only respond "Properly" when the "Left Eye" is affixed on the inside of the back of the ball, and he/she is on "Balance," only then will the true growth appear. For the golfer to advance continuously at an even pace, he/she must not settle for something that does not achieve consistent scoring ability. Now, when he/she is on the course, the only thing that matters, other than following the rules, is what score was shot. (Nothing else matters).

The will to win energizes the golfer to greater heights, from the hours and hours of practice, practice, and more practice. Now, let us cut through the "Crag Mire" of confusion that holds the "average Golfer" from ascertaining or grasping the concept learned. This phase is about using the information learned, allowing it to free the mind by keeping it occupied with pertinent "Data" and a calm demeanor. He/she will quickly become aware of how much outside interference he/she was allowing themselves to be distracted instead of staying into and upon "Routine and Set-Up."

The true "Glue" is practice and playing with a "Tempo!" I

personally found the lack of is not only a "Swing Killer" but a "Game Killer."

What he/she must always remember is that the only "Opponent" he/she is up against is the "Golf Course," manage it properly, and also keep the "Highs and Lows" under control. The golfer cannot allow the "Emotions" to pull him/her into the "Trap" of being overly "Dramatic" or "Celebrating" while losing "Focus." Now he/she realizes that golf is not "Hard" it is "Complicated." "Execution" demands that he/she practices and plays with a tempo and becomes aware that you cannot play "behind or in front of oneself," so he/she must stay in the "Moment," one shot at a time. Using the "Routine," "Set-Up," and "Tempo" to complete "Each Shot." In the "Execution" phase, the entire exercise is about "Meshing the "Aptitude" and "Execution" while maintaining calm by using the "Attitude" to hold them all together. Remember, the "Physical" will break the "Mental" down faster than the opposite. The "mental" phase of golf takes a toll on the "Committed" and "Uncommitted" golfer.

Golf is just like life: "If it's not winning, it's not working." The way and what he/she practices will make an enormous difference in the pace of his/ her development he/she is seeking.

It is my sincere hope that the information that has been shared has been the "Mental" awareness and information needed to make the difference in the readers' better understanding of the "Proper" information to improve one's game.

"STAY FOCUSED!"

Horace L. Mitchell

My name is Horace Mitchell, son of Evans and Geneva Mitchell. I was born in the small town of Bastrop, Louisiana, in Morehouse Parish. The reason this is important is the training I received growing up from home and throughout the community. This gave me a "Winning Attitude" in anything I pursued.

The average golfer starts playing golf in one of four to five ways:

- Has a family member or friend that plays.
- Happens to go to a Putt-Putt or Driving range for fun.
- Decides to learn as a hobby or job-related.
- Introduces the family because all can play.
- Uses Golf to obtain scholarship opportunities for the children.

Now that is out of the way, let's get down to the "Nuts and Bolts."

"The Average Golfer" generally plays this game along the lines that they were introduced to the game. The only way that changes is if he/she finds they have developed a passion for the game or needs it for business.

I would like to give you a little insight into myself so maybe you can understand the reason why this is necessary. I started golf in 1974 at the age of 28 years old, never really thinking about golf as a younger man, and certainly not as a means of bettering oneself. I really must thank my wife for sending me to the "Driving Range" just to give me something to do other than bothering her while working. If not for that, this would never be happening.

Once at the range, my first thought was: *I guess the range can get ready to buy more "Balls" because these babies are out of here.* Well, any golfer can tell you the outcome of that exercise. Sixteen (16) buckets later, I was hitting the driver (the ones I hit) about 25 to 75 yards and out of breath, hands sore, but although I was totally disgusted, I was more determined than ever. After a short time at the range, the local golf pro by the name of "Mickey" approached me, and what he said made all the sense in the world. "Young man, I've been watching you from the first day you came to the range. What I notice is a dedication and drive that I rarely see. I am an instructor; my lessons are $7.00 per half hour, but you will learn the proper mechanics to strike the ball."

I took twelve lessons from Mickey. Then I asked, "When do you think I am ready for the golf course?"

Mickey said, "You have been ready for a week, but I was waiting for you to ask."

Then I enquired about the proper equipment to buy. Once that was done, away to the course, I went. Palmer Park Golf Course was the only golf course I had noticed, mainly because it was less than ten minutes from home. I'll never forget the first time I stepped foot on the "Tee" at Palmer Park. Never having played a round of golf in my life, I was amazed and awed by my unfamiliar environment. There were three gentlemen on "Tee," and one of them asked if I would like to join them to make it a foursome. Man, this was great; there was no need to find someone to play with. What I didn't realize until after the introductions, and once I explained that this was my first time "ever" on the golf course, that is when it was explained to me that there were certain wagers taking place, but if I didn't want to be involved, I did not have to. Being a gambler at heart, I asked for an explanation of the process and how much, then away we went. To my "Astonishment" and to the "Amazement" of the elderly gentlemen who invited me, not only did I win all my bets but shot 46, the very first time I played nine holes. The next thing that awed me was the fact that I won the money, but they would not allow me to buy anything in the "Club House." In the culture I was accustomed to prior to golf, the participants were not happy campers after any loss. What impressed me the most was the stylish attire all the men and women wore and the awesome golf bags and clubs. Soon, I began to visit Palmer Park every chance or opportunity I had. Golfers are easy to befriend, so that fits my character fine. Within that season, someone told me if I wanted my game to be better, I should go to the nine-hole "Belle Isles Golf Course," so I took that advice.

After a week or so, I met the four other beginner golfers who changed each of our golf lives and are friends to this day. The early days at Palmer Park taught me one of the most valuable lessons that is still with me today: "Only hit the shot you are confident you can hit." This became increasingly clear to me because the pressure of playing with "Low or No" funds did not allow me to have the affordability to try anything other than what I was sure I could hit and control.

Please bear with me; this is for the average golfer, so in the event the reader questions any thought process derived through this text, it is clearly and purely "MINE." Throughout my many years of playing the game of golf, I have never seen anyone become proficient at golf who was not a lover of "Practice."

Palmer Park turned out to be the perfect place for learning to play because anytime you teed off, two things were happening: one - there was a "medal bet," and two - there were skins, so you had to stay aware of your score all the time. With Palmer being open and flat on the front nine, this allowed you to develop a recovery game with mostly "Bump and Run." Also, the greens on both sides of the course are unusually small once the front has been gotten under some kind of control. Now, let's continue to the "Back Nine;" this is an entirely different course from the "Front Nine." On this side of the course, all the "Greens" are "Elevated," with only two of the nine not "Slopped" with trouble over the back of most of them. This requires the golfer to learn how to elevate the ball flight with the approach shot or pitching and chipping game. Palmer Park had small greens; the golfers that used Palmer Park as their "Home Course" tended to be better than average chippers and putters wherever we played and also had a higher percentage of hitting greens than the golfers on his/her level. Learning this under the strain of pressuring yourself to learn the golf swing while staying at the driving range. Not realizing the progress that is "Expected" from the hours and hours invested. It is not like I wasn't playing better, but the golfers that I was grouped with were called the "Garbage Train;" we were the true "Duffers." Once again, everyone had "Bets" with everyone. Sometimes, there would be as many as 40 golfers in our Saturday and Sunday games that were always away from Palmer Park. Once I found myself being whispered about among the other "Garbage Train" participants, I knew the time had come to move on or stay a "Garbage Trainer" forever. From my former lifestyle, I knew the only way to move to another level is to put the level you are on at risk. This is when I discovered the importance of "Attitude" and how it seems to "Handicap" not only the ability to improve the golf game but your "life." The love I had developed for the game, even at this early stage, was consuming me, and the quest to improve my "Skill Sets" and scoring ability was truly overwhelming, to the point I began to take lessons, read books, and as soon as videos surfaced, I was all in. To say this did not help would be an understatement. Anytime you set out to learn how far you are away, a strange thing happens: you are in awe of the realization of how close you really are. This revelation was my first recognition as to why one must seek out "Stronger Competition." The only way to know if what you are working on is proper that can only be proven when it is "Tested," other than that, it's impossible to know. It took a long time, and I would venture to say it was unnecessarily eventful because of my belief in hidden secrets and quick fixes or easy cures such as new equipment, gadget clubs, and new swing tips. This is when it dawned upon me that my approach had to be not wrong but improper! "Humble" means to have low self-value or esteem. This word is always used in connection with sports because it is hard to improve yourself until you allow the admittance of one's own weaknesses and fears. Only then can we realize that "No One Is all that and a piece of Bubble Gum." At this point, "factual information" began to reveal itself because, now, my attitude was open. That brought on a new sense of understanding. As I began playing stronger golfers, it quickly became clear what the weakness in the average golfer's game was and is; I could see it in myself. My "Attitude" was fine; it was the "Aptitude" that was really lacking. This one point of recognition was the next positive feeling about my progress up to this point. Another thing I noticed was that because I was playing stronger competition, the "Focus" required was much different than with my prior competitors. This is when the effort was directed into building as strong of a "Short Game" as I could develop. The continuous practice of my "Putting and Chipping, turned out to show instantly. The more I began to "Focus" on the detail of "Ball Placement" off the "Left Instep" and then watch the "Right Instep" as I stepped away, was "Enormous." The thing that makes this system work is training oneself to become "Left Eye" dominant. I hope I do not lose you as I go through this especially important phase of enlightenment. Once I moved to chipping and pitching, my realization and understanding of the information from the many lessons taken started to click. My "Scoring" got lower but inconsistent. To me, this was the point where the "Mental" aspect of the game became involved. I started being "Aware" of things that had not been thought about before. My summation as to why this happens is that the total "Focus" has been striving to become a good, if not great, "Ball Striker." Then he/she becomes "Tunneled Visioned" and seems to refuse to accept that it's not the inability to strike the ball that's not allowing them to progress at the rate "Expected," but the lack of a "Short Game" that is equal supersedes the ability to strike the ball. The first thing I began to realize was that the word "Expectation" was the "Killer of Dreams" and keeps the individual from dealing with "Right and Wrong." There is no such thing as "Right or Wrong" in the game of golf; there is only "Proper or Improper." This is the only way the improvement one is seeking can be accomplished because you are only dealing with "Results." The words "Right or Wrong" are only used in "Law," whether man's law or biblical law. The words "Right" and "Wrong" are used in these areas because they deal with things that have no "Degrees" of "Lying and Death." Once a "lie" is told, there are no "Degrees" to it; it is "Just a Lie," and once anything is "Dead, it's Dead," there are no "Degrees" that is only to clarify the sentencing phases in the "Judicial System and Religious Sects." I found that one of the main reasons for me holding myself back was paying too much attention to my opponents and then "Focusing" on myself and managing my own development as a "Scorer" instead of just being a good "Ball Striker," but not "Winning." I had always wondered why every coach I've ever had and every good to great athlete I have ever heard talk about the road to achieving any measure of success, whether a man or woman, they all use the word "HUMBLE" until you begin to deal with the first vestige of pushing beyond ones "comfort level" and admit that there might be a proper way to approach becoming a better "Scorer," only then will you discover why this game "Humbles" you. It has always been a mystery to me since the meaning of "Humble" is to have a "low opinion of oneself." Why is it that he/she must reach that level to obtain the true level they seek? After I was "Humbled" by all the "Failed" attempts and hours of practice, I became "Aware" of the "Mental Errors" that were not allowing me to learn to "Focus" on the important "Components and Structure" of the 'Set-Up and Stance." The thing the "Average Golfer" should know but keep in mind, is that the swing is built around the "Grip," not the other way around. It took me some time to understand that the only way I could repeat the process was to build a solid "Routine," once constructed, I was showing vast improvement. One day, on the phone with a close friend from home, he was talking about the "Routine Drills" our coaches made us practice over, repeatedly and again, until we never had to second guess ourselves in the heat of the "Battle." I am proud to say my high school won everything we participated in the "Double A" competition in the state of Louisiana. Now it "Clicked." Hah. "Routine." This is what I have been seeing in the pros and all the stronger golfers not recognizing not only what was happening but the importance of it. Even the "Average" golfer who takes the time to use the same "Routine" will play and score better than his/her contemporaries.

The game of golf is the image of "Life" in every aspect.

A- You enter the game totally void of any knowledge.

B- How or who introduced you to the game will mean a lot to the developmental process and growth.

C- The more he/she puts into practice the "Routine" and "Set up" but also incorporates a "Tempo" to the process, the more growth can be seen.

The game of golf is not "hard," it's "Complicated." It's the reason the game can "Never" be truly "Mastered," only for so long. If there is a "Routine" involved, the golfer that sticks the closest to his/her practice "Routine" will find themselves being a consistent "Winner" on the level they are playing

The Mental Guide for The Average Golfer

on. Mentally, once a certain level of consistency has been achieved, he/she must "Focus" on his/her ability to keep that "Focus" for 10 or 19 holes. The greatest lesson I learned was how much attention I wasn't paying and how involved I was in someone else's game or something else going on around me. There was never enough time spent staying involved with my own "Problems." The theory was devised for building "Focus" and creating thought processes in between shots and moving to the next Tee. Once on the course, there is no time to allow the "Mental" to stray or get caught up in swing thoughts in the middle of the match. It's said that "an idle mind is the devil's workshop." I think all can "attest" to that because of the nature of our human experience, we cannot leave well enough alone. Once the mind has its focus on scoring, the entire golf game takes on new meaning. At this level of "Awareness," the clarity of why there is no such thing as "Right or Wrong" in golf begins to become clear. The "Mental" side of golf is the reason the average golfer runs into "The Wall." This is the point where the decision will be made: "To yourself by yourself, how far you want to go." This game demands that you play a certain number of times under different conditions on different courses. Since it is natural for the game to build confidence in oneself, this can only be achieved by proving to yourself that the "Routine" that is being used supplies the results you are after. The average golfer probably won't ever shoot below 90. I had wondered why none of the instructors I took lessons from when I was learning ever talked about the "Mental," nor did they stress the importance of keeping the entire set-up process "between" the "Foot." The golfer who can keep themselves from the highs and lows that go along with every round of golf will find they will have a more productive round than usual. "Mentally," one must train themselves to become "Left-Eye Dominate" for "Right-handers" and the opposite for the "Left-handers." The underlying cause for the "Average Golfer" not being more proficient is the lack of "Putting/

Horace L. Mitchell

Chipping and Pitching" practice; this means he/she gets weaker the closer to the "Green" they get. The "Short Game" and "Putting" practice will take strokes away from the golfer's game right away. This is entirely about the "Mental Approach," so in the event the reader is not following this trend of thought, it is the very reason for me reaching out to give the golfers who are looking for a better and stronger game insight into how to carry out that goal. Golf is the one game that, once a person falls for the game, confronts you with a different challenge than ever before. The overriding issue with learning golf is, from the time he/she begins, it's a challenge to not get caught up in only pursuing the physical aspect of golf when ultimately the only "Roadblock" is the inability to remove oneself from getting in one's own way. It's the "Mental" that controls the entire golfing experience; the ability to play up to a certain point can be achieved in a reasonable amount of time, but it generally ends there. For the average golfer, this is where he/she starts to get entrenched into believing that it's their swing that is not allowing them to progress, especially at the rate they expect from the work being done. The only thing that I've found over the years was what a different approach meant. I truly had to "Think About It." When I did that, I sat down and thought about it. All I could see was me spending 90% of my time working on the swing and the ability to keep my ball safe, but only 10% on learning to finish the hole. There is an impossibility for he/she to raise their level of scoring until he/she becomes a "Solid" chipper and putter, without the ability to complete the hole after being able to consistently get into position and not be able to leave with "Par," will destroy a golf game. The only way I've found, the surest way to improve the ability to score, is to work harder on the "Short and Intermediate" game instead of putting all the pressure on the "Long Game." In the game of golf, the only thing that's counted is the score. Other than following the rules, nothing else matters. Once the "Mental Aspect" is involved, the ability to "Focus" becomes optimum. To create the "Focus" needed, a rude awakening occurs. You begin to realize it takes "Focus" to create greater "Focus." Now let's have a little "Fun," the reason I say this is because even though I have said this is not an issue for "Argument or Debate," I make no claims to be professionally schooled or trained in the "Psychology" of golf. Everything I talk about is what it took for me to become a professional "Average Golfer." Unless the "Average Golfer" is pursuing a professional career, this information should be an asset to improving the scoring facet of his/her golf game. No matter what level he/she plays golf at, that will be the level of aspiration for improvement. Learning to control the "Mental" aspect allows the golfer to understand it's the structure of the "Set-Up" that begins to deal with the body's "Weight Shift" and the importance of becoming "Left-Eye" dominant and between the "Feet." The strength of any athlete's ability is the ability to keep "Balanced" when executing. This is why learning to "Focus" must be crucial to one's scoring ability. "Mentally," he/she cannot afford to allow his/her thoughts to "Travel." There are too many "Obstacles" facing him/her, and there is never enough time to be distracted by anything from the outside world.

Golf starts the golfer to realize that the greatest asset one can have is "Awareness," just like in the game of life, "Everything" matters. There are no "insignificant" things. Remember this one phrase: "The Stronger the Routine, the Stronger the Golfer." No matter what the sport, the athlete who has the strongest routine and is willing to practice, practice, and practice more will more than likely surpass his/her competitors. The "Mental" approach is the only thing that can create true growth and put it all together. The ability to "Control" one's ever-changing emotions is the "Bedrock" of his/her consciousness of the level of "Awareness" needed to be consistent at "Ball Striking" round after round. The concept of being a good "Striker" of the ball is what the "Average Golfer" is looking to become, but what is not understood is not how well he/she "Strikes" it when the "Mental and Short Game" is not solid. Even when you are the "Average" golfer, you can be more efficient and have more fun because winning at golf gives the golfer confidence beyond the most satisfying experiences in one's "Sports" activities. It takes a lot of time to become proficient at any phase of golf. Because of the four sections of the game, it is difficult to bring them together, and when it looks as if one might have carried out the task, it falls apart again. It is my contention that the omission of spending time on the mental aspect, as well as the psychological stress of scoring, makes it hard to truly keep the "Focus" necessary to do the things practiced. Understand that every human has constructed some kind of "Routine" for everything and anything; anyone who believes or thinks that this doesn't apply to them is one of the main reasons learning or training oneself the process to be a consistent scorer is so hard! Mentally everyone is up against the same obstacles, why is it that you can attend the same school receiving the same education, but no one does the same thing with it? This only deals with one's ability to point oneself in the direction they are pursuing. The earlier an individual has his/her mindset to "Focus" on whatever their aspirations are for their future, the greater the probability and possibility of achieving that goal!

Please don't take the last paragraph as relating to the game of "Golf," but the game of "Life!" The major disconnect in the game of golf is the "Endless Fight" the golfer has, keeping the "Mental" aspect in check throughout the round by training himself/herself to play one shot at a time. The "Mental" is what must be trained to stay focused on welding the "Four" components together. The reason the word welding was used is to get the reader to understand how the words that are used must always yield an atmosphere or confidence. I have played with all levels of golfers since 1974, and not once have I seen a golfer maintain any measure of consistency without some kind of "Routine," no matter how weak.

I think it was "Arnold Palmer" who said, "As long as you live, you never stop learning this game." The reason for this is why they have different "Tee Boxes" because the distance one can compress the ball diminishes as we age. The greatest mistake that has been clear to me is the "Average" golfer doesn't want to "Give Up the Ghost;" the body changes whether your mind does or not. Golf is one of the only games played for a lifetime that the entire family can indulge in. Keep in mind that the game of golf should primarily be fun, no matter how he/she plays.

I sincerely hope that the message that was aired in this text will be beneficial to the reader.

Everything talked about is the disconnect between a golfer and his/her ability to play consistently better golf no matter what level they want to achieve. There is no such thing as a "Bad" instructor, but there are plenty of lesser informed. Understand, when the "Average" person seeks instruction, they only want to be proficient at hitting the ball, so that's what they are taught. By the time they become good enough to go to the course, they haven't learned anything about "Scoring." The main goal of the game is to become proficient enough to at least threaten the scorecard. It has always been a mystery to me when a golfer makes the statement that they aren't too keen on playing certain courses because they are too "Easy!" Once again, the 'Mental' approach to the game has taken on an egotistical attitude, and this golfer only plays the game with "Expectation" nine times out of ten. The golfer that has that sentiment is a "Double Digit" handicap with a little better game than his or her playing partners. "Mentally," an "Athlete" can't ever afford to think or feel that the challenge ever gets "Easy." After an individual learns to be consistent in hitting the ball and has developed the ability to break a 100 on the course, to get better, he/she will need to learn to "Focus" on an elevated level of some form of routine. My suggestion is to seek the proper instructions to keep from getting locked in bad habits and beliefs that will keep him/her back for years, if not from now on. No matter how well the golfer can strike the ball, the ability to "Score" has to be the total focus other than keeping the physical in shape to keep it from straining the mind. Most of the golfing community are weekend or recreational golfers, but this game has a personal side like no other, and in my experience, there is almost no better feeling than executing a solid golf shot; I know it's what hooked me. The most enjoyable but enlightening aspect of the entire experience was the key to finding "Consistency" in my scoring and not shooting well one day, but maybe not again for a few days or maybe a week. This must be the most frustrating part of learning this game. For some reason, neither the "Mental" aspect nor approach is touched on when a person begins to learn this game; they only go on the concept that hitting the ball is going to be the "End all Do all," and then the famous words "I Got It," which means you will never hit another good shot that day playing or practicing. The game of golf is "Strictly" about "Scoring," so hitting the ball is especially important, but being proficient at "Putting, Chipping, and Pitching" and watching the improvement in scoring is important. Also, the consistency of the other parts of the game comes together.

To play a decent round of golf takes 18 holes of "One Shot" at a time from the number one "Tee" until the 19th hole; this is why golf is so difficult because it's imperative that the "Focus" and "Concentration" stay on keeping the golfer into the task at hand. It has become open knowledge that the "Mental" challenge is the greatest challenge for the "Athlete." The field of sports psychiatry has grown rapidly. Over the years, God has blessed me with the ability to reach the young people around me differently than most. To date, I can testify to the fact that because of our involvement, "Student and Coach" are better and stronger by it. One of my proudest moments was when I was chosen to the 2011 class of the Michigan Chronicle's "Men of Excellence," awarded each year for the contributions to the community.

In conclusion, my sincere wish is the information in this text that I personally had to write to cover "For the Average Golfer," the one area of instruction that most have never thought of to strengthen one's golf game and become a better scorer. This information should be helpful in any facet of the game the average golfer is pursuing.

Stay Focused!

HORACE L. MITCHELL
(Coach Dent)
Hollywood Golf Institute
Master Golf Educator
United States Golf Teachers Federation
Licensed – 2021

Thank You Note

There is not a lot of time in this life, but we seem not to realize it until the journey is almost complete. Trying not to be a victim of not making the effort to leave something behind, on this journey, I must thank the men and women in my life who have allowed me to enjoy the trip.

First, I would like to think of my wife. If not for her sending me to the driving range just to get me out of her hair, this would not be happening. It has always been a pleasant memory whenever I think of "Mickey," my first golf professional from "Stacy's Driving Range." I honestly believe taking those lessons in the beginning is truly the reason I developed at a rapid pace in comparison to my peers. Benny Davis (FIRST Black PGA professional in the state of Michigan), from Rackham Golf Course, was the next pro I went for lessons, and from the time I saw him swing, I knew what a real golf swing should be. After the information was obtained, I then met Charles Forster (Brother). What I learned from Brother was the importance of the shoulder turn, and he informed me that my shoulder turn would be the reason I had a chance to build a strong golf swing. I always admired and respected Brother's instructing skill and analytical approach. Tommy Harden was one of the better pros that I watched play and win or finish high in the tournaments he entered. Tommy Harden was the pro who made me understand the importance of setting up off the left heel to establish my wall behind the ball.

Horace L. Mitchell

The golf instructor really broke through the fogginess and confusion that was not giving me progress, not at the level or rate I was seeking, and not from the work put in. Trying to unlock that magic formula or find a quick cure.

Mr. Junior Simmons, whom I had breakfast with most mornings, one morning I was asked if I knew that he was also an instructor. "I see you taking lessons and getting information from everywhere; why haven't you ever taken a lesson from me? My fee is $7.00 dollars per half hour."

I explained to him that it had never occurred to me or come up, but here is the money for three lessons. "Now, all I need to know is where I fit into your client base, and tell me when we start." That turned out to be the best investment I ever made.

Mr. Simmons was a disciple of the "Clock System" while improving posture and weight distribution. Bingo, the light came on. By already working on developing a routine or system to obtain some kind of consistency, what Junior Simmons taught me moved my game forward at an alarming rate. I got much better.

Since this is to acknowledge the people who are responsible for helping me create a strong, dependable golf game, here are just a few:

Junior Simmons- Golf Instructor
Norman Collier – Georgia Boy
Jimmy Jones – Left-hander
Phil Dean – Silver Fox
Curtis Walker – National Champ
Lee Willams- Little Lee (Pro)
Horace White – Gino (Pro)
Eddie Leonard- (Pro)

I could go on and on, but these were the gentlemen who gave me the basic structure and foundation to construct a solid routine, a positive mindset, and an approach. As I am putting pen to paper, I cannot give enough credit to my friend and talented colleague, Mr. Jessie Jacobs Jr. One never knows the impact one will make or be until an effort is made in an area where no matter what is given, there is nothing expected in return. I learned this from my "Friend." I must thank the Hollywood Golf Institute for allowing Mr. Jacobs and myself to train the young students and enjoy the best times of our lives. Thank the University of Maryland Eastern Shore for allowing the Hollywood Golf children to be the first to tee up on then the new "Driving Range." Seven of those children years later attended UMES's PGM program to achieve a PGA card. My one regret is that Mr. Jessie Jacobs Jr. is not here because of his involvement and contributions to the instruction and molding of the children's "Attitudes." Also, to see me do what was suggested by him six years earlier. His strong knowledge of the basics was one of his best assets. By the way, because of that, he was also my instructor. Jessie showed me another level of understanding and compassion.

Because of the love received from my family and friends and my faith in God, I have been allowed to pursue my passion. For this, I am truly thankful.

www.ingramcontent.com/pod-product-compliance
Lightning Source LLC
Chambersburg PA
CBHW050728010526
44107CB00009B/778